WE
THE PEOPLE
CHIEF JOSEPH

Library of Congress Cataloging-in-Publication Data

Rothaus, James.
  Chief Joseph.

  (We the people)
  Summary: A biography of the Nez Percé chief who led
his people on a long trek to escape the injustices of the
United States government and never stopped fighting for
equality.
  1. Joseph, Nez Percé Chief, 1840-1904—Juvenile
literature.   2. Nez Percé Indians—Biography—Juvenile
literature.   3. Nez Percé Indians—History—Juvenile
literature.   4. Indians of North America—Northwest,
Pacific—History—Juvenile Literature.   [1. Joseph,
Nez Percé Chief, 1840-1904.   2. Nez Percé Indians—
Biography.   3. Indians of North America—Biography]
I. Title.   II. Series: We the people (Mankato, Minn.)
E99.N5J67   1987   970.004'97   [B]   [92]   87-24578
ISBN 0-88682-158-4

WE
THE PEOPLE
CHIEF JOSEPH

NEZ PERCE INDIAN LEADER
(1840-1904)

JAMES R. ROTHAUS

Illustrated By John Keely

CREATIVE EDUCATION

CHIEF JOSEPH

Hundreds of years before the white explorers came to America, an Indian tribe made its home in the beautiful valleys to the west of

7

the Rocky Mountains. Here, in lands that are now part of Oregon, Idaho and Washington, the Indians saw that the Great Spirit had entrusted a very special place to them.

They would never be hungry. Plump salmon splashed in the rivers. Deer tracks were everywhere in the hills. Delicious berries, nuts and roots sprang from the fertile earth. At times, the skies above were alive with noisy flocks of geese and ducks.

The Indian people felt fortunate. They vowed to respect the animals, the rivers, the earth and each other. Because honor and self-respect were important to them, the Indians were true to their word in peace—and brave in battle.

By the time the white French traders came into their country, the tribe had become large and prosperous. The friendly braves approached the whites on beautiful spotted ponies that we now call Appaloosas. The traders named the Indians Nez

Perce, which is French for "pierced nose"—a custom of the tribe.

The Nez Perce chiefs could see that the white men had knowledge and tools that could benefit Indian people. They asked for white teachers, and so missionaries and their families went to the Nez Perce.

Many of the Indians became Christians. They lived side by side with the whites and called them their brothers in faith. One of the most important Christian chiefs was Old Joseph, who lived in the Wallowa Valley. About 1840, a son was born to the chief.

The missionaries called the boy "Young Joseph." When he was five or six years old, he went to the mission school. Like all children, he loved to play and get into mischief. But his father was quick to remind Young Joseph that the day would soon come when he would have to grow up and be a leader.

In 1847, trouble came to the white missionaries. Deadly sickness infected the Cayuse tribe, neighbors to the Nez Perce. The Cayuse blamed the white people, and killed 12 of them. The U.S. Army was sent to punish the Cayuse.

Old Joseph watched the missionaries flee. "Perhaps the white religion is not so strong after all," he thought. "When trouble comes, the missionaries' faith is in their feet rather than their hearts."

Several years went by. The chief and his family were no longer

Christians. They had returned to the old religion of their people. They called the Earth their mother and loved the land.

When he was ten years old, Young Joseph went off alone to pray to the Great Spirit, the Maker-of-All, just as all young men of his tribe did. As he prayed, he saw a vision of himself as a great chief. He heard a voice give him a name: Thunder-Rolling-in-the-Mountains. It was a name of great power.

At first, Young Joseph was frightened and confused by the vision. He was just a boy, but now he also felt like a man inside. He prayed for the courage to live up to his new name. He asked for wisdom to find and follow the right path.

The years went by. Young Joseph grew older. From his father he learned to be a great hunter and warrior. And like his father, he was wise and honorable. But he worried when more and more white people poured into the Indian lands. The settlers chopped the trees, built

14

fences across old Indian trails, and fouled the rivers. Some gave liquor to the Indians so they could cheat them or make fun of them. Surely, more trouble lay ahead.

In 1855, the U.S. government made a treaty with the Nez Perce. The tribe promised to live only on a reservation in the Wallowa Valley. In return, the government would pay money, food, and supplies. Even though the government did not keep its promises, the Nez Perce kept theirs. They stayed at peace with the whites for more than 15 years. They still hoped that someday all people—red and white—would learn to be brothers.

But now greedy gold miners and settlers invaded the reservation.

They knew it was wrong, but they made the excuse that the friendly Nez Perce were just "savages." And savages didn't deserve to own anything.

Old Joseph, the chief, was dying. Sadly, he called his son. "The time has come," the old man said. "Now you will be the chief of these people. They look to you to guide them. You must stop your ears if white men ask you to sign a treaty and sell your home. A few more years and the white men will be all around you. They have their eyes on this land. But never forget my dying words! This country holds your father's body. Never sell the bones of your father and your mother."

The words of his father were like an arrow in Young Joseph's heart. For the second time in his life, he felt frightened and confused. Once again, he prayed for wisdom and courage.

In 1871, Thunder-Rolling-in-

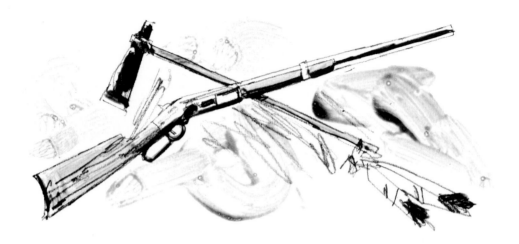

the-Mountains became chief of his people. The white leaders called him Chief Joseph, and this is the name that has gone down in history. From the very beginning, the young Nez Perce leader faced a difficult task. To keep the peace, he knew he would have to cooperate with the white government. But to keep the promise made to his father, he would have to defend the land—with his life, if necessary.

Chief Joseph's worst fears came true. More white ranchers came to live in the Wallowa Valley Reservation. Finally, the government came to make a new treaty with the tribe. Chief Joseph's people were told to move north, to another reservation.

Joseph listened respectfully. Then he tried to make them understand. "This land is our mother," he explained. "We cannot leave her."

"You must move," the government agents said. "We promise you new land, a new mother."

But Joseph refused. The chief remembered all the old promises that had been broken. Why should he believe new promises?

In May of 1877, the U.S. Army

was sent to the valley to force the Nez Perce onto the new reservation.

Chief Joseph saw that many warriors were ready to fight. He tried to prevent bloodshed by urging the people to pack up and leave. Sad and angry, they left their beautiful home forever.

Burdened by children, old people, cattle, ponies and goods, they could only travel very slowly. They met Chief White Bird's band at Rocky Canyon and made camp.

That night, the young braves came together with fire in their eyes. "The white men say one thing, but they mean another," they cried. "Keeping the peace has left us homeless. Even our chiefs are humbled and afraid."

Joseph could not stop them from riding out. The hot-headed young warriors murdered four white men, then came back to tell the chiefs:

"Now you will have to fight with us. Soon the soldiers will be here. Prepare for war! Prepare for war!"

For years, Joseph had worked for peace. But now the people rose up in fury. All the other chiefs wanted war. Joseph, their leader, could only follow.

Bands of warriors attacked white settlements. Army troops sent after the Nez Perce rode into an ambush at White Bird Canyon. The army forces were crushed by the red men. It was the worst white defeat since the Battle of the Little Big Horn the year before.

The happy Indians celebrated their victory. But Joseph knew that a black future lay ahead. A thousand soldiers would be coming. What would happen then?

Now Chief Joseph took command once more. The battle skills learned at his father's knee were not forgotten. Joseph proved to be the military equal of General O.O. Howard, who was sent out to capture him. Howard had about 600 experienced soldiers. Joseph had perhaps 200 warriors, with 400 more women, children, and old people. It should have been easy for the white army to subdue the Indian band.

Instead, Chief Joseph seemed to outwit the white general at every turn. The Indians won fight after fight, but Joseph knew that time was on the army's side. The Indians' only hope was to escape.

For the third time in his life, Joseph prayed for the wisdom to find and follow the right path.

Again and again the white army tried to trap the fleeing Nez

Perce. But the warriors fought the
troops and won, while the people
escaped. All over the United States,
people read about the war and mar-
veled at the skill of the red men,
led by Chief Joseph. He took them
over high mountains, through track-
less wilderness. For four months they
traveled, until winter was upon
them. Then, just 30 miles from the

Canadian border, Chief Joseph and his people were surrounded. It was the end.

Chief Joseph rode forward alone toward General Howard and General Nelson A. Miles. With dignity, he gave them his rifle. Then he said:

"Tell General Howard I know his heart . . . I am tired of fighting. Our chiefs are killed . . . It is cold and we have no blankets. The little children are freezing. We have no food. Hear me, my chiefs. I am tired. My heart is sick and sad. From where the sun now stands, I will fight no more forever."

White men had promised Chief Joseph that his people would be returned to their own country.

But once again, the white promise was broken. The Nez Perce were sent to Kansas, then to the Indian Territory (now Oklahoma). Many died there.

Finally, in 1885, Joseph and his band went to a reservation in the state of Washington. The chief spent the rest of his life trying to make the government fulfill its promises. He died September 21, 1904, still waiting.

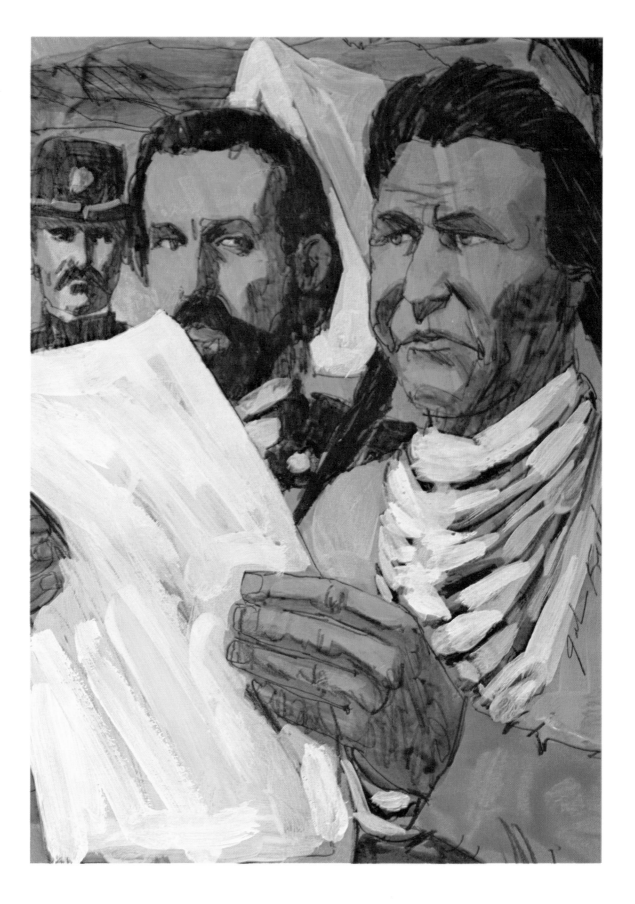

WE THE PEOPLE SERIES

WOMEN OF AMERICA

CLARA BARTON
JANE ADDAMS
ELIZABETH BLACKWELL
HARRIET TUBMAN
SUSAN B. ANTHONY
DOLLEY MADISON

INDIANS OF AMERICA

GERONIMO
CRAZY HORSE
CHIEF JOSEPH
PONTIAC
SQUANTO
OSCEOLA

FRONTIERSMEN OF AMERICA

DANIEL BOONE
BUFFALO BILL
JIM BRIDGER
FRANCIS MARION
DAVY CROCKETT
KIT CARSON

WAR HEROES OF AMERICA

JOHN PAUL JONES
PAUL REVERE
ROBERT E. LEE
ULYSSES S. GRANT
SAM HOUSTON
LAFAYETTE

EXPLORERS OF AMERICA

COLUMBUS
LEIF ERICSON
DeSOTO
LEWIS AND CLARK
CHAMPLAIN
CORONADO

Date Due
